New York State

Government & Counties websites

by

Paul F. Davis

The state of New York, known as the empire state because of its vast wealth and resources, has 62 counties accounting for and governmentally managing the great state. Amassing over 20 million people, the state of New York is the fourth most populated state in the United States and home to New York City, the most populated and economically powerful city in the nation. New York City is arguably the cultural, financial and media capital of the world.

New York is one of the original thirteen colonies that formed the United States. New York is home to the United Nations, Asian Society, Statue of Liberty, Broadway, Times

Square, Central Park, Niagara Falls, Grand Central Station and some of the world's most iconic and frequently visited tourist attractions.

New York is a global epicenter for diversity, cuisine, vibrant culture, music, creativity, entrepreneurship, business, innovation, sustainable eco-friendly real estate, environmentally conscious urban planning, social and ethnic awareness for which reason it is a cherished UNESCO World Heritage Site.

New York state is home to two outstanding Ivy League universities: Cornell University located in Ithaca and Columbia

University located in New York City. Thirdly, New York University is the most chosen higher education institution by international students when they study abroad. All three prestigious universities in the state of New York rank among the top 50 universities in the world.

Moreover, the state of New York has approximately 200 colleges and universities, among which is the ever expanding State University of New York, among the largest university system in the United States.

Source:

https://en.wikipedia.org/wiki/New_York_(st

ate)

Paul F. Davis is a graduate from New York University, where he earned a Master degree in Global Affairs, while studying in lower Manhattan near City Hall at the Woolworth Building within NYU's Center for Professional Studies.

Paul also worked at the World Trade Center in New York City during the rescue relief effort following the attack during the first days after September 11, 2001. Paul has lived in both Brooklyn and Queens, where he enjoyed the vibrant culture and cuisine.

Paul has traveled throughout New York City on foot, by subway and air via helicopter. Paul has traveled to and went snow skiing in Lake Placid (a former winter Olympic site), The Thousand Islands and Niagara Falls (bordering Canada). Paul's daughter is half Canadian, her mother originating from Ontario, just north of the state of New York.

Paul's father was a real estate appraiser, broker, and home builder. Thus, Paul grew up with a keen understanding of real estate law, state and county jurisdiction, building codes and the nuances of pulling a permit when constructing and remodeling homes with his father. Paul also earned a Master degree in Law from Michigan State College of Law, where he earned a jurisprudence award within the field of Administrative Law, related to federal government agencies, policy and protocol.

For this reason, Paul as a world traveler and someone who has also traveled throughout New York and the United States, took interest in researching the state of New York to ascertain the many government and counties' websites to assist politicians, entrepreneurs, business and community leaders, real estate developers, urban planners, families, citizens and others seeking to relocate to the area to easily find the government offices and officials in authority who can best serve their needs and the respective agencies therein who can advance their interests.

This timeless and priceless resource will be an asset to governments, multinational companies, CEOs, executives, business and community leaders, entrepreneurs, real estate developers, urban planners, aspiring and seasoned politicians, nonprofit organizations, churches, social service workers and grant writers eager to network with brokers of power and partner with those with positions of influence capable of bringing about positive change within their respective areas of interest.

Sometimes with elections come power shifts and changes in government. Thankfully, most government websites remain the same and do not change despite changes in governmental leadership. Nevertheless, sometimes due to cyber security issues, distrust and insecurities in leadership; politicians may propose, opt, or pursue website url changes to feel more at ease regarding possible data breaches, prevent hacking and give them more peace of mind amid political opposition (who perhaps previously ran the website, mined and managed the online data). For this reason, I respectfully apologize if in the future a website previously in operation suddenly ceases to work, as such is beyond my control.

Nevertheless, if and when a county website

was tough to locate, I often added a couple of

websites to track different aspects of county

government operations and their respective

offices to at minimum lead you in the right

direction (and often therewith provide some

valuable bonus sites with unique data that will

further enlighten you as to the region, the

economic opportunities therein, future

development and its potential).

"A wise man will hear, and will
increase learning; and a man of understanding
shall attain unto wise counsels" (Proverbs 1:5).

"Give instruction to a wise man, and he will be
yet wiser: teach a just man, and he will
increase in learning" (Proverbs 9:9).

 "The wise in heart shall be called prudent:
and the sweetness of the lips
increase learning" (Proverbs 16:21).

"The heart of the wise teaches his mouth, and
adds learning to his lips" (Proverbs 16:23).

"Give attendance to reading, to exhortation, to
doctrine" (1Timothy 4:13).

Paul F. Davis is a global business consultant, an international educator (licensed in Florida and California) and UCLA certified University and Career Counselor. Paul speaks for governments, companies and universities worldwide on a number of topics.

PaulFDavis.com
EducationPro.us
Tinyurl.com/PaulFDavis-Books
RevivingNations@yahoo,com

Please email Paul to check his availability to speak in your city and/or provide consulting services.

Hereafter are 19 pages
of websites for the state of New York
and its respective counties
to easily access.

New York Government & Counties Websites

New York State
https://www.ny.gov/

U.S. Department of State in New York
https://www.state.gov/states/new-york/

New York State Government
https://www.usa.gov/state-government/new-york

New York Governor
https://www.governor.ny.gov/#:~:text=Kathy%20Hochul%20is%20the%2057,New%20York's%2026th%20Congressional%20District.

New York Attorney General
https://ag.ny.gov/

https://www.naag.org/attorney-
general/letitia-
james/#:~:text=Letitia%20%E2%80%9CTish
%E2%80%9D%20James%20is%20the,the%2
0State%20of%20New%20York.

New York State Assembly
https://nyassembly.gov/

New York State Comptroller
https://www.osc.state.ny.us/local-
government

City of New York
https://www.nyc.gov/
https://twitter.com/nycgov
https://www.facebook.com/NYCGov/
https://www.linkedin.com/company/city-of-
new-york/

New York City Government Agencies
https://www.buildingcongress.com/industry-
links/New-York-City-Government-
        Agencies

New York State Unified Court System

https://ww2.nycourts.gov/lawlibraries/nyoffi
cesagencies.shtml

New York State Education Department
http://www.nysed.gov/

**New York State Local History and
Government**
https://www.pbslearningmedia.org/collection
/new-york-state-and-local-history-and-
goverment/

New York – Urban Institute
https://www.urban.org/policy-centers/cross-
center-initiatives/state-and-local-finance-
initiative/projects/state-fiscal-briefs/new-
york

Counties of New York State
https://www.p12.nysed.gov/repcrd2005/links
/nycounty.shtml

How New York Government Works
https://www.ny1.com/nyc/all-
boroughs/politics/legislature-faqs

New York City as the Seat of Government
https://www2.gwu.edu/~ffcp/exhibit/p2/

League of Women Voters' of New York
https://lwvny.org/structure-of-new-york-state-government/
Albany County – New York
https://www.albanycounty.com/
https://www.ny.gov/counties/albany
https://www.albanyny.gov/
https://www.linkedin.com/company/albany-county-ny/
https://www.facebook.com/McCoyAlbanyCou
ntyExec/ https://www.albany.org/

Allegany County – New York
https://www.alleganyco.gov/
https://www.alleganyco.com/

Bronx County – New York
https://bronxboropres.nyc.gov/
https://www.ny.gov/counties/bronx
https://www.ny.gov/counties
https://www.bronxda.nyc.gov/html/home/ho
me.shtml
https://data.nysed.gov/profile.php?county=3

2

https://www.introducingnewyork.com/bronx
https://bronxhistoricalsociety.org/
https://ww2.nycourts.gov/COURTS/12jd/BR
ONX/Surrogates/index.shtml
https://portal.311.nyc.gov/article/?kanumber
=KA-02877

Broome County – New York

https://www.gobroomecounty.com/

Cattaraugus County – New York

https://www.cattco.org/

Cayuga County – New York

https://www.cayugacounty.us/

Chautauqua County – New York

https://chqgov.com/
https://www.co.chautauqua.ny.us/
https://www.ny.gov/counties/chautauqua
https://www.tourchautauqua.com/

Chemung County – New York

https://chemungcountyny.gov/

Chenango County – New York

https://www.co.chenango.ny.us/

https://www.ny.gov/counties/chenango
https://www.loc.gov/item/2012593650/

Clinton County – New York
https://www.clintoncountygov.com/
https://www.ny.gov/counties/clinton
https://www.adirondack.net/maps/countyma
ps/clinton/ http://cceclinton.org/
https://www.inaturalist.org/places/clinton-
county-ny-us

Columbia County – New York
https://www.columbiacountyny.com/

Cortland County – New York
https://www.cortland-co.org/

Delaware County – New York
https://delawarecounty.org/
https://www.delcony.us/
https://www.facebook.com/delconygov/
https://www.ny.gov/counties/delaware
https://www.co.delaware.ny.us/departments/
ltc/ltc.htm

Dutchess County – New York
https://www.dutchessny.gov/

https://www.facebook.com/DutchessCoGov/
https://www.ny.gov/counties/dutchess
https://ww2.nycourts.gov/courts/9jd/dutches
s/index.shtml
https://dutchesstourism.com/

Erie County – New York

https://www2.erie.gov/home/
https://www4.erie.gov/
https://www.ny.gov/counties/erie
https://www.facebook.com/ErieCounty/
https://twitter.com/ErieCountyNY/
https://www.linkedin.com/company/erie-
county/

Essex County – New York

https://essexcountyny.gov/
https://www.facebook.com/EssexCountyNYG
overnment/
https://www.ny.gov/counties/essex
https://www.adirondack.net/maps/countyma
ps/essex/ https://essexnewyork.com/
https://www.co.essex.ny.us/

Franklin County – New York

https://www.franklincountyny.gov/
https://www.franklincony.org/

Fulton County – New York

https://www.fultonmontgomeryny.org/
https://www.fultoncountyny.gov/
https://www.ny.gov/counties/fulton
https://www.facebook.com/VisitFultonCount
yNY/
https://www.facebook.com/fultoncountyarea
news/
https://www.loc.gov/resource/g3803f.la0004
97/

Genesee County – New York

https://www.co.genesee.ny.us/

Greene County – New York

https://www.greenegovernment.com/
https://www.facebook.com/GreeneCountyNe
wYork/
https://www.ny.gov/counties/greene
https://greenecountyedc.com/
https://travelhudsonvalley.com/explore-
counties/greene/
https://www.loc.gov/item/2013593222/

https://www.loc.gov/resource/g3803g.la000
500/

Hamilton County – New York
https://www.hamiltoncounty.com/

Herkimer County – New York
https://www.herkimercounty.org/

Jefferson County – New York
https://co.jefferson.ny.us/
https://ww2.nycourts.gov/courts/5jd/jefferso
n/family/index.shtml
https://www.ny.gov/counties/jefferson
https://www.facebook.com/profile.php?id=10
0064861383405
https://www.facebook.com/groups/15725798
09627946/
https://www.inaturalist.org/places/jefferson-
county-ny-us
https://www.loc.gov/item/2013593068/

Kings (Brooklyn) County – New York
https://www.nyc.gov/site/kcpa/index.page
https://www.brooklyn-usa.org/

https://www.ny.gov/counties/kings
https://ww2.nycourts.gov/courts/2jd/kingscl
erk/index.shtml
https://data.nysed.gov/profile.php?county=3
3
https://www.nychealthandhospitals.org/locat
ions/kings-county/
https://www.loc.gov/item/2013593268/

Lewis County – New York
https://www.lewiscounty.org/
https://naturallylewis.com/
https://ww2.nycourts.gov/courts/5jd/lewis/s
urrogate/index.shtml
https://linkinglewiscounty.com/
https://ccelewis.org/
https://www.facebook.com/groups/lewcoeve
nts/ https://www.loc.gov/item/2013593274/
https://www.dec.ny.gov/outdoor/55783.html
https://www.lewiscountysoilandwater.com/
https://www.lcgh.net/
https://www.nny360.com/news/lewiscounty/

Livingston County – New York
https://www.livingstoncounty.us/

Madison County – New York

https://www.madisoncounty.ny.gov/

Monroe County – New York

https://www2.monroecounty.gov/

Montgomery County – New York

https://www.co.montgomery.ny.us/

Nassau County – New York

https://www.nassaucountyny.gov/
https://www.ny.gov/counties/nassau
https://www.nassauda.org/
https://ww2.nycourts.gov/COURTS/10JD/nassau/district.shtml
https://abc7ny.com/place/nassau-county/
https://www.bls.gov/regions/new-york-new-jersey/ny_nassau_md.htm

New York (Manhattan) County – New York

https://www.manhattanda.org/
https://ww2.nycourts.gov/courts/1jd/surrogates/index.shtml
https://www.nysd.uscourts.gov/
https://www.ny.gov/counties/new-york
https://www.nypl.org/smallbiz/services/item

/156877
https://www.newyorkschools.com/counties/n
ew-york.html
https://www.nationsonline.org/oneworld/ma
p/USA/new_york_map.htm
https://forecast.weather.gov/MapClick.php?z
oneid=NYZ072
https://portal.311.nyc.gov/article/?kanumber
=KA-02877

Niagara County – New York
https://www.niagaracounty.com/

Oneida County – New York
https://ocgov.net/

Onondaga County – New York
http://www.ongov.net/
https://www.ongov.net/
https://www.ongoved.com/
https://www.linkedin.com/company/ononda
ga-county/
https://www.ny.gov/counties/onondaga
https://www.facebook.com/OnondagaCounty
/
https://ww2.nycourts.gov/courts/5jd/ononda
ga/supremecounty/index.shtml

https://www.onlib.org/
https://onondagacountyparks.com/
https://www.loc.gov/item/76692660/

Ontario County – New York

https://ontariocountyny.gov/
https://www.co.ontario.ny.us/

Orange County – New York

https://www.orangecountygov.com/
https://www.facebook.com/OrangeCountyGovernment/
https://orangeny.com/
https://www.ny.gov/counties/orange
https://www.ocnyida.com/
https://travelhudsonvalley.com/explore-counties/orange/
https://orangetourism.org/
https://www.inaturalist.org/places/orange-county-ny-us

Orleans County – New York

https://www.orleansny.com/

Oswego County – New York

https://www.oswegocounty.com/

Otsego County – New York

https://www.otsegocounty.com/

Putnam County – New York

https://www.putnamcountyny.com/
https://www.facebook.com/putnamcountygov
/
https://www.ny.gov/counties/putnam

https://ww2.nycourts.gov/COURTS/9jd/Putn

am/putnamsupreme.shtml

Queens County – New York

https://www.queensbp.org/

Rensselaer County – New York

https://www.rensco.com/

**Richmond (Staten Island) County –
New York**

https://www.statenislandusa.com/

Rockland County – New York

https://rocklandgov.com/

St. Lawrence County – New York

https://www.stlawco.org/

Saratoga County – New York

https://www.saratogacountyny.gov/

Schenectady County – New York

https://www.schenectadycounty.com/

Schoharie County – New York

https://www.schohariecounty-ny.gov/
https://www4.schohariecounty-ny.gov/

Schuyler County – New York

https://www.schuylercounty.us/

https://ww2.nycourts.gov/courts/6jd/schuyler/county/index.shtml

https://www.ny.gov/counties/schuyler

https://www.facebook.com/schuylerhistory/

https://data.nysed.gov/profile.php?county=55 https://www.flxgateway.com/

https://cugir.library.cornell.edu/catalog/cugir-007987

https://www.mytwintiers.com/schuyler-county/

Seneca County – New York

https://www.co.seneca.ny.us/

Steuben County – New York

https://www.steubencountyny.gov/

https://www.ny.gov/counties/steuben

https://ww2.nycourts.gov/courts/7jd/Steuben/Surrogate/index.shtml

https://www.dec.ny.gov/outdoor/46088.html

https://data.nysed.gov/profile.php?county=57

https://www.facebook.com/SteubenCountyOES/

https://cugir.library.cornell.edu/catalog/cugir-007989

https://www.fingerlakes.org/explore/counties/steuben

Suffolk County – New York

https://www.suffolkcountyny.gov

https://suffolkclerk.com/

https://www.ny.gov/counties/suffolk

https://www.scnylegislature.us/

https://ww2.nycourts.gov/courts/10jd/suffolk/county.shtml

https://abc7ny.com/place/suffolk-county/

https://www.suffolkcountyhistoricalsociety.org/

Sullivan County – New York

https://www.sullivanny.us/

Tioga County – New York

https://www.tiogacountyny.com/

Tompkins County – New York

https://tompkinscountyny.gov/

Ulster County – New York

https://ulstercountyny.gov/

Warren County – New York

https://www.warrencountyny.gov/

Washington County – New York

https://washingtoncountyny.gov/

Wayne County – New York

https://web.co.wayne.ny.us/

Westchester County – New York

https://www.westchestergov.com/

Wyoming County – New York

https://www.wyomingco.net/

Yates County – New York

https://www.yatescounty.org/

Paul F. Davis is a global business consultant, an international educator (licensed in Florida and California) and UCLA certified University and Career Counselor. Paul speaks for governments, companies and universities worldwide on a number of topics.

PaulFDavis.com
EducationPro.us
Tinyurl.com/PaulFDavis-Books
RevivingNations@yahoo,com

Please email Paul to check his availability to speak in your city and/or provide consulting services.